VENUS RE-DEFINED

SCULPTURE BY RODIN, MATISSE AND CONTEMPORARIES

TATE GALLERY LIVERPOOL

CONTENTS

SPONSOR'S PREFACE

We believe in contributing to the cultural life of the area in which we operate: our sponsorship of *Venus Re-Defined* reflects not only our tradition of support for the visual arts in the North West, but also our desire always to promote the best in quality and beauty.

Our roots are very much in the North West with shops in Altrincham, Chester, Liverpool, Manchester and Southport; we are delighted to be associated for the first time with Tate Gallery Liverpool, working together to enable audiences from outside London to enjoy the best of the National Collection of modern Art. We are particularly proud to be involved with a display showing the Matisse *Backs* outside London for the first time.

We hope that you will enjoy the display, and that you will take the opportunity to return to it time and again over the coming year.

David M Robinson
Managing Director
David M Robinson Jewellery

DAVID·M·ROBINSON
DESIGNER AND MANUFACTURER OF EXCLUSIVE DIAMOND AND GOLD JEWELLERY

DIRECTOR'S PREFACE

Venus Re-Defined has been selected from the collection of the Tate Gallery by Judith Nesbitt, Exhibitions Curator, with the aim of showing the changing use of the female nude as a subject for sculpture. All the sculptures were made in Paris in a fifty-year period from 1890, a time when artists began to break free of the powerful traditions of the Ecole des Beaux-Arts and the Salon.

The starting point for the display is Rodin who, in the words of the critic Leo Steinberg, 'unsettles the obvious and brings to sculpture that anxious questioning for survival'. Rodin's 'anxious questioning' is exemplified in several distinguished sculptures most generously lent to the Tate Gallery by the Victoria and Albert Museum, works which immeasurably enrich the Tate's own holdings.

Rodin's questioning attitude to his subject underpins the whole display. Nowhere is this more evident than in Matisse's remarkable series of four bronze *Backs*, shown for the first time outside London.

Included are works in bronze, lead, and wood by Rodin, Matisse, Maillol, Renoir, Zadkine, Archipenko, Lipchitz, and Laurens. These sculptors, many of whom were familiar with each other and with each other's work, represent the extraordinary range of possibilities which opened up for sculpture in this period, in the after-shock of Rodin: 'primitivism', classicism, Impressionism, Cubism, and Surrealism – none of which labels evokes the thrill with which they exercised this new freedom.

Alongside recorded statements by these sculptors, we are pleased to have contributions from contemporary artists, Cathy de Monchaux, Antony Gormley, and Alison Wilding, through whose eyes we can see Venus, muse and nymph afresh.

Nicholas Serota
Director, Tate Gallery

Lewis Biggs
Curator, Tate Gallery Liverpool

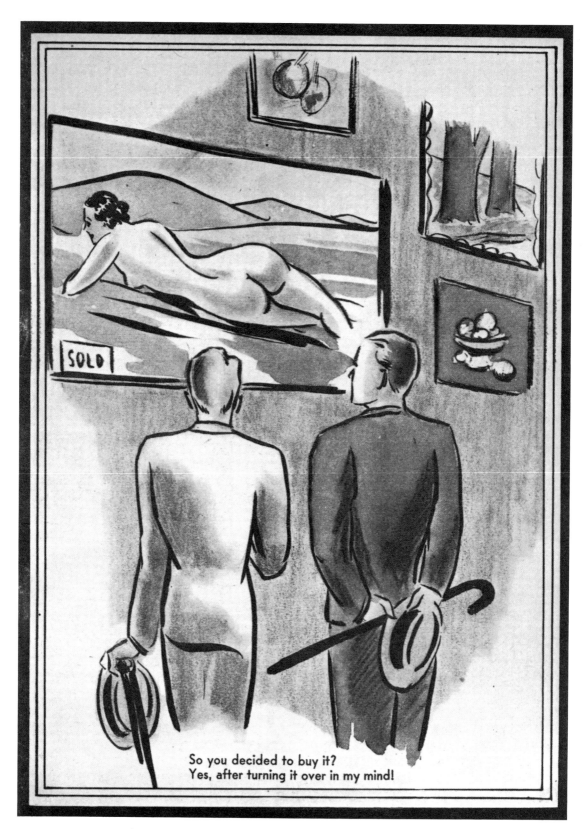

fig 1 Cover illustration to *Allen Jones: Work on Paper* exhibition catalogue,
Waddington and Tooth Graphics, 1976

INTRODUCTION

Judith Nesbitt

Beauty queens exist to be looked at, and Venus, the Goddess of love, and beauty queen of Antiquity, has long since had a special relationship with artists. Venus, in the guise of earthly models, has serviced artists' needs in a multitude of ways: looking sexy, keeping still, pouting and posing, reflecting onto them some of her Olympian glory, and no doubt occasionally making a cup of tea.

Venus Re-Defined is a selection of sculpture which takes a span of time – from the end of the nineteenth into the first part of the twentieth century, and a place – Paris, fulcrum of the modernist movement in art, and cuts across the 'isms' of classicism, 'primitivism', Cubism, Surrealism, to trace the survival of that most traditional of subjects: the female nude. In the process, the sculpted Venus undergoes what we might regard as plastic surgery. She is made to change shape, size and function to fit her for the modern era. 'We of today', wrote Matisse, 'are trying to address ourselves today – now – to the twentieth century – and not to copy what the Greeks saw and felt in art over two thousand years ago. . . It makes no difference what are the proportions, if there is feeling'.

This is a display of sculpture of women by men. Until 1900, women were not admitted to the Ecole des Beaux-Arts (the most prestigious Art School in Paris) and one of those who fought for this, the sculptor Camille Claudel, is not represented in the Tate collection. Women such as Claudel had to study privately and she chose to study with Rodin, who was much preoccupied (though not exclusively) with representing the female nude. Several of the sculptors in the display, Matisse and Maillol in particular, concentrated almost entirely on the female nude.

The body has always been a primary subject for the sculptor, from pre-historic cave drawings to the statues of ancient Greece and Rome. In the nineteenth century, when this display begins, an academic sculptor's main source of work was official commissions to produce monuments and adorn public buildings with heroic bodies. (Painters, able to work at less expense, and sell more easily to a private market, had always enjoyed greater artistic freedom than sculptors).

fig 2. ALEXANDRE CABANEL *The Birth of Venus* 1863

Most of the artists represented in this display studied at the Ecole des Beaux-Arts, where students had to draw from plaster casts of antique statues before they were allowed to draw from life. In this way artists were taught to improve upon nature by looking to an ideal of classical beauty: to re-align curves, and smooth over the irregularities of the life model's body.

In representations of the female body, this idealising process resulted in such fantasy females as seen in the painting of *The Birth of Venus* by the French artist Alexandre Cabanel (fig 2, above), one of three pictures of Venus bought by Napoleon III from the 1863 Salon. Cabanel's Venus is 'born' perfectly formed and fresh from the beauty parlour, it would seem. She rolls in upon the waves, writhing with pleasure, to a fanfare from Cupid and a few of his friends. Having abandoned everything except her powers of vision, she is able to send an inviting wink and nod to her male admirers. In this way the viewer is invited to take possession of the female body, a male prerogative parodied in the cartoon illustrated here (fig 1, opposite).

Compare the Cabanel Venus to Rodin's *Crouching Woman* (p 21), made just a few years later, and related to his studies for *Iris, Messenger of the Gods*. The depiction of the female body could not be more different (allowing also for the difference in media). In place of the coy 'kiss me quick' of Cabanel's Venus is the frank sexuality of a woman's body depicted in athletic

9

fig 3 ANONYMOUS: GREEK
*Venus de Milo c*100 BC

The subject of Maillol's *The Three Nymphs* (p 23) derives from classical mythology in which nymphs were female spirits who inhabited nature. Maillol admired the 'Archaic' art of pre-Hellenistic Greece which emphasised solid, architectural mass in its depiction of the human body. Although the female body is presented in Maillol's sculpture with similar serenity, it also shows his attraction to the rounded, solid bodies of the peasant women he liked to use as models. The pose of the woman in *The Three Nymphs* is (with small variations) the same one repeated three times, allowing the viewer to see the whole figure – front and back simultaneously. This classical trio takes the form of *The Three Graces*, but Maillol stressed their difference: 'they are too solid to be graces' he said. The trio form a self-contained and self-sufficient whole which no mere mortal could enter.

Zadkine's *Venus* (p 34) treats a classical subject in a more unconventional manner. Venus is given shape in a tree trunk, her ideal beauty translated into a totem-like sculpture, the sensuality of the rounded grain played against the angularity of her body. Despite the avant-garde use of direct carving (which in any case is consciously beautiful in a way that, for example, Picasso's early carved wooden figures are not) Zadkine chooses a standard studio pose for the model – the left arm bent at the elbow, hand on head. *Venus* is a work which combines artistic traditions across cultures and centuries. It is a supreme effort to reconcile a classically derived, conventional studio pose with the re-discovered technique of direct carving, spurred by contemporary interest in non-Western art, and in Zadkine's case coupled with an interest in Romanesque carving.

In his series of four bronze reliefs *Back I – IV* (pp 28 - 31), Matisse made a similar transition across traditions, but in stages, and in separate sculptures over a period of twenty years. It seems that, at varying intervals, Matisse resolved his ideas by working in three dimensions. Hence they bear a close relationship to his paintings. *Back I* corresponds to the surviving drawings which show a model posed in the studio against the wall. Using the model's back as a subject for art was not unknown but was uncommon. What, for Matisse, was so fascinating about the back? Formally it would seem that the more continuous forms of the female back (without the distraction of face, breasts, pudenda etc) allowed him to pursue greater unity

movement, legs splayed in defiance of false decorum. Possessed of her own energies, her dynamic pose is a flagrant display of freedom, as much for the sculptor as for the woman represented. (For the model it was probably a limb-numbing experience). In this example as in all his work, Rodin pushes the limits of sculpture to meet the challenge of the youthful, aging, wilful, emotional, sexual, excitable human body. To him, that challenge was best expressed through his treatment of the female body, which often has a sexual charge.

One critic remarked at the time that 'what other sculptors indicate with a slight touch, Rodin's fingers scoop right out'. If Rodin's modelling of the body subverted traditional ideas of beauty and finish, it was not accepted by the younger generation who followed. Maillol was for a time a student of Rodin, and admired his achievement but like many of his contemporaries, chose to take a very different course. Ruth Butler, Rodin's biographer, writes: 'Every sculptor who came to Paris after 1900 had to come to terms with Rodin . . . and they all had to work away from him. . . The direction they took . . . was towards simplicity, stillness, and a new kind of balance'.

between the body and the wall, or in actuality, the image and the block of bronze. This he achieves, by stages so perplexed but purposeful, in the final version, *Back IV*. Here the studio pose is disbanded and in its place is a massive figure, the exotic pony tail used to anchor the upper half to the bottom: a visual and volumetric equivalent to the trunk-like legs. The studio model, who struggled to establish her position in relation to the wall, is now integral to the slab – transformed into object rather than subject.

The intellectual rigour of Matisse's practice, always searching for greater sculptural logic, cannot be found in any other painter-sculptor in this display. Renoir in fact only took up sculpture when he was an old man crippled with arthritis, working with an assistant, and pointing his instructions with the aid of a bamboo rod. When he came to making his over life-size *Venus Victorious* (p 24) he had firm ideas, however, about her shape. He employed a favourite model, Maria, a young woman from Essoyes, but didn't want his sculpture (in his words) 'to stink of the model', and so wrote to a friend asking him to measure the vital statistics of classical statues but not, he specified, the Venus de Milo 'who is a big gendarme' (shown then, as now, in the Louvre, armless, fig 3, left). Renoir, it seems, preferred more rounded shoulders and a wider pelvis for his opulent *Venus*, who holds the prize of the golden apple, as proof of her unmatched beauty. Evidently he enjoyed the opportunity to join with Paris, Prince of the Trojans, in judging Venus' beauty. He corrected a sketch of the projected Venus, making the belly and hips heavier, and raised the breasts a few centimetres. He also remodelled the face, giving her a 'make-over' in a pseudo-classical style.

Laurens worked to no such prescription. He said: 'When I begin a sculpture I have only a vague idea of what I want to do. For instance, I have the idea of a woman or of something related to the sea…I provide a title right at the end'. *Autumn* (p 38) is the title he gave to one of his last large bronzes, a reclining nude, inviting writers ever since to liken her to plump fruit ripening in the sun. The woman's limbs are indeed like inflated aubergines mutating to the point of imminent explosion. Having worked in a Cubist style, Laurens felt under no obligation to make the form of his sculpture follow the actual shape of a model, and in this case lifted both legs into the air to

fig 4 Cartoon *Devant la Venus D'Archipenko*, Paris, 1912

balance the upraised arm in a gravity-defying stunt.

Within the span of this display it is possible to see the strict conventions of official 'Salon' sculpture overturned with such vigour and variety that we might feel some sympathy for the two women faced with a sculpture of Venus by Archipenko, in a cartoon in a French journal (fig 4, above): 'Is this really the sister of the one in the Louvre?', asks one, to which her friend replies, 'Yes, but not by the same father'.

I was taken to Rodin's studio in the rue de l'Université, by one of his pupils who wanted to show my drawings to his master. Rodin, who received me kindly, was only moderately interested. He told me I had 'facility of hand', which wasn't true. He advised me to do detailed drawings and show them to him. I never went back. Understanding my direction, I thought I had need of someone's help to arrive at the right kind of detailed drawings. Because, if I could get the simple things (which are so difficult) right, first, then I could go on to the complex details; I should have reached what I was after; the realisation of my own reactions.

Henri Matisse on Auguste Rodin

My work discipline was already the reverse of Rodin's. But I did not realize it then, for I was quite modest, and each day brought its revelation... Already I could only envisage the general architecture of a work of mine, replacing explanatory details by a living and suggestive synthesis.

Henri Matisse

Rodin is the genius who has given movement to his whole epoch; he is a man whom I could never be... Rodin was a god.

Aristide Maillol on Auguste Rodin

I know nothing in modern sculpture so absolutely pure.

Auguste Rodin on Aristide Maillol

Nature is deceptive. If I looked at her less, I would produce not the real, but the true. Art is complex, I said to Rodin, who smiled because he felt that I was struggling with nature. I was trying to simplify, whereas he noted all the profiles, all the details; it was a matter of conscience.

Aristide Maillol

The particular does not interest me. What matters to me is the general idea.

Aristide Maillol

Maillol's sculpture and my work in that line have nothing in common. We never speak on the subject. For we wouldn't understand one another. Maillol, like the ancient masters, proceeded by volume and I am concerned with arabesque like the Renaissance artists. Maillol did not like risks and I was drawn to them. He did not like adventure.

Henri Matisse on Aristide Maillol

I took up sculpture because what interested me in painting was a clarification of my ideas. I changed my method and worked in clay in order to have a rest from painting, where I had done all that I could for the time being. That is to say, it was done for the purposes of the organisation, to put order into my feelings and find a style to suit me. When I found it in sculpture, it helped me in my painting. It was always in view of a complete possession of my mind, a sort of hierarchy of all my sensations, that I kept working in the hope of finding an ultimate mastery.

Henri Matisse

Cubism was not a school, an aesthetic, or merely a discipline – it was a new view of the universe. Cubism sought a new way to represent nature, a manner adequate to the age. Cubism was essentially a search for a new syntax. Once this was arrived at there was no reason for not employing it in the expression of a full message. This is what I feel I have done and what I am still trying to do.

Jacques Lipchitz on Cubism

I did not take from Cubism, but added to it.

Alexandre Archipenko

It is not exactly the presence of a thing but rather the absence of it that becomes the cause and impulse for creative motivation. This process exists in nature as latent force and is the fundamental creative inducer of new organic life. Nature creates that which is not yet there.

Alexandre Archipenko

Picasso used to say to me, about Cubism: 'Why did we abandon it? It was so magnificent'.
At the time of Cubism, we all thought along the same lines. But we couldn't go on making *papiers collés* all our lives.
We gave all we could give in that common endeavour. After that each of us had to go his own way.

Henri Laurens

I look for stability even when representing movement. Movement doesn't disturb the impression of calm my sculpture is meant to give.

Henri Laurens

In a sculpture it's necessary for the voids to have as much importance as the masses. Sculpture is, above all, a taking possession of space, a space limited by forms.

Henri Laurens

I aspire to a ripeness of form. I should like to succeed in making it so full, so juicy, that nothing could be added.
When I begin a sculpture, I only have a vague idea of what I want to do. For instance, I have the idea of a woman or of something related to the sea.
Before being a representation of whatever it may be, my sculpture is a plastic act and, more precisely, a series of plastic events, products of my imagination, answers to the demands of the making. That, in short, is all my work amounts to.
I provide a title right at the end.

Henri Laurens

Sculpture, as we understand it today, is one of our happiest acquisitions. But sculpture can also be a bowl made out of stone, a knife, made by the Mayas, out of those dark green crystals. It is also an object. And this object can have all that you expect of a work of art, something which can emanate and speak to you. A speechless language, the something that moves you all of a sudden.

Ossip Zadkine

When men came to the necessity of doing an object which would last, they always put into it something of their love, of their necessity, of their *temperature*, of their energy. And this energy is still in the object and it emanates. Without this energy – this specific energy – the object would not emanate anything at all.

Ossip Zadkine

The female body in sculpture has been taken as a ground to be possessed, idealised or broken and this display is full of examples of this kind of treatment, from the classical idealisations of Maillol to the impositions of Lipchitz.

Rodin, while he used all these strategies, is different in one, critical, respect: he realised that there is little value in using the body except to express feeling and he empathises with it (as we are invited to do) – even if it is a battleground in which old beliefs cannot hold. This is most clearly evoked in *The Muse*. Here Rodin allows sculpture to express a nakedness that escapes the conventions of the nude. As viewers we are asked to empathise with this inner state exposed in outer form. The gesture of touching the breast (made even more poignant by the arm having been amputated) has a psycho-sexual function expressing self-possession but also a longing for connection. This is also clear in the *Large Head of Iris*, where he is able, in spite of the distancing effect of bronze, to make the sympathy between clay and flesh carry the yearning of the body for the earth.

Rodin is the liberator of the body in sculpture. He set it free from the restraints of history so that it could become a ground for feeling. Matisse's reclining figure carries this sympathy – but the rest of the work in the display looks too much like sculpture. For me working a hundred years later, Rodin offers the greatest challenge to re-integrate the body within itself.

Antony Gormley

Venus: the name for a goddess, a celestial body, and man-made objects evoking desire. Our need to touch is a powerful one; touching and holding are a temporary possession. I speculate that 25,000 years ago those tiny Neolithic Venuses were held in the hand. Denied to us, touch must be compensated for by the pleasures of looking.

Matisse worked on his series of *Backs* over a period of 21 years. In *Back IV* he reshaped his landscape as inexorably as the slow eroding glide of a glacier carving out valleys and accreting moraine. This simple geography makes a massive totemic slab. It is Matisse's monument to femaleness. In her newness and rawness she surpasses the previous *Backs*. Her terrain covers that of the Cerne Abbas giant in Dorset, and that of the Venus of Willendorf. She is implacable, ceremonial, stubborn. We stand behind her, never in front of her.

On the whole, women artists don't create gods though I am reminded that Mary Shelley's creation in her book, *Frankenstein or the Modern Prometheus*, was last seen on an ice-raft heading towards his own funeral pyre at the North Pole.

Alison Wilding

Having been asked to think about these sculptures, it is Rodin's *The Muse* which comes first to mind. It reminds me of the time I first saw it.

I can see it very clearly now in my mind's eye. The tilt of the body, that vast empty space between waist and arm. That solid thigh, vertical, tree-like. The torso bent to this almost but not quite impossible angle, but with something curvaceous going on at the same time, which I saw as a serpentine locked into a grid of straight lines.

It's strange to try and describe it in words when in fact what I want to do, even now, is to draw it. When I first saw it I drew it over and over again, obsessively trying to work out why it was not just what it appeared to be.

As I write, I remember that bent knee, the lump on which the foot rested and the casting lines dividing the stomach, diagrammatically. From the back of the body (well, it *was* the back, although there was really no back or front) the lines travelled over a kind of landscape. It had this solid arse, on the end of the straight leg which propped the torso, and where the shoulders were was a really immense flat plane. I remember the fierce jut of the elbow which twisted the plane of the shoulder forward and back to the front again. It created this weird feeling in my stomach – a moving experience maybe – but maybe it was just the assertiveness of the angle.

It was the arm which stretched up at the same time which made it happen, of course, but the place where the elbow of the bent arm shifted back over this really solid, empty space of the waist, punched me out emotionally somehow. Maybe it was because it was a measured space, not merely formed by an imaginative scooping.

I first saw this piece in 1979. I had a rendezvous in Paris with my lover, who was there, but somehow finally absent to me. The awkwardness of reality had overcome our imaginative expectations.

I escaped to the Musée Rodin, that monument to maleness. I question now how I could love so much the work of a man whose relationship to his models is so problematic for us today. I suppose there is something, even now, abstractly seductive about the idea of the intellectual and erotic relationship between sculptor and model that lies beyond morality in the non taboo land of the imagination.

Looking back now, I realise that what I couldn't understand about its potency then, was that the very amoral, almost fantasy-like existence of the artist, combined with this intense forming of the object (which was not merely emotive - more formal and engineered) allowed him to infuse it with that sense of unbridled lust that I'd lost that morning. Somehow he had formalised that tense aching desire, into that gap between elbow and waist, the wrench of the arm, the strength of the vertical leg, the curving serpentine interfaced with the assertive straight lines and the scar of the casting. To leave an object gasping with the expectation of being on the edge of becoming. . .

Cathy de Monchaux

CATALOGUE OF WORKS

Compiled by Judith Nesbitt

Unless stated otherwise,
dimensions are given in millimetres,
height before width before depth

AUGUSTE RODIN
1840–1917

French sculptor, draughtsman and engraver, born in Paris. Studied at the Petite Ecole 1854–7, failed to get into the Ecole des Beaux-Arts; worked as an ornamental mason and at the Sèvres porcelain factory. Visited Italy in 1875 to study Michelangelo. In 1878 he exhibited *The Age of Bronze* in Brussels and Paris, and was accused of having cast it from life: not only did it look like a slavish copy, but was also 'a most commonplace individual'. He was commissioned to make doors for the Musée des Arts Décoratifs in Paris: the project, known as the *The Gates of Hell* took more than twenty years and contained 180 figures; many of these were also enlarged as separate sculptures. His work was much criticised, especially his monument to the nineteenth-century writer Balzac, which was refused by its commissioners, the Société des Gens de Lettres. Had his first substantial exhibition with Monet at the Galerie Georges Petit, Paris, in 1889, but was only properly recognised (and then lionized) after he organised a large exhibition of his work during the Paris International Exhibition, 1900. Died at Meudon. The works he owned were presented to the French government, and form the collection of the Musée Rodin in Paris.

Cybele
*c*1904–5
Bronze
1600 x 1190 x 830
Lent by The Board of Trustees of the Victoria & Albert Museum 1993
L01697

This figure was also originally designed as part of *The Gates of Hell*. The enlarged plaster was exhibited in 1898, and was the first of Rodin's 'fragments' shown as a sculpture in its own right rather than as a study.

The work was exhibited again, in the Paris Salon of 1905, this time titled *A Figure*. Rodin's decision to show truncated and fragmented figures as complete works was influential on the younger generation of sculptors such as Maillol, Matisse, and Lipchitz. Since he was slow with *The Gates of Hell*, however, the exhibition of rough, unpolished work like this was taken by the public as proof that Rodin was incapable of finishing anything.

The sitter was the well-known model, Madame Arbruzzese, and the sculpture is sometimes named after her. It was called *Cybele*, after the Greek Goddess of the earth, on its exhibition in London in 1914.

AUGUSTE RODIN
The Muse
*c*1896–7
Bronze
1460 x 768 x 571
Lent by The Board of Trustees of the Victoria &
Albert Museum 1969
L00514

Originally derived from a fauness on *The Gates of Hell*,
where it appears on the right of the tympanum, *The
Muse* is a variant of *The Inner Voice* (a title by which it
is also known) intended for the *Monument to Victor
Hugo*. However, the fact that it was separately cast and
signed, and presented by Rodin to the Victoria and
Albert Museum in 1914 along with several other
works, indicates his satisfaction with it as an independent work.

Typically, Rodin's ideas for the *Monument to Victor
Hugo* underwent several stages of evolution. Invited
by the French Ministry of Fine Arts to design a monument to the French poet, Rodin's original proposal
was for a naked Hugo, seated on a rock, surrounded
by three muses, where the prototype for the present
figure appeared, in Rodin's conception, as 'an ideal
figure'. This proposal was considered inappropriate
for the Pantheon building, but Rodin was invited to
continue with it for a possible site in the Luxembourg
Gardens. When he exhibited it at the Salon de la
Société Nationale in 1897, the three allegorical figures had been reduced to two, symbolising in Rodin's
words, 'voices that whisper into the poet's ear': *The
Tragic Muse* and *The Inner Voice* (the latter title suggested by Hugo's collection of lyric poems, *Les Voix
Intérieures*). Rodin eventually abandoned the idea of
the two muses, exhibiting a marble figure of Hugo
alone at the Palais Royal in 1909.

The Inner Voice was an enlargement from the small
bronze cast of *Meditation*, derived from *The Gates of
Hell*. When Rodin took up this figure again for the
Monument to Victor Hugo, he enlarged it dispropor-
tionately in the head and feet, threatening the figure's
equilibrium.

Rodin's practice of enlarging individual figures from
a smaller model allowed him to reconsider the right-
ness of proportion within the sculpture. *The Muse*,
exhibited at the Salon of 1890, demonstrated his
audacity. He told Ambroise Vollard, his dealer:

'I am giving away one of my secrets. All those trunks
you see there, so perfect in their forms now that they
no longer have heads, arms or legs, belonged to an
enlargement. Now, in an enlargement, certain parts
keep their proportions, whereas others are no longer
to scale. But each fragment remains a very fine thing,
Only, there it is! You have to know how to cut them
up. That's the whole art'.

In its long gestation, *The Muse* underwent many
changes, not least the severing of the arms. At one
stage, when the arms were intact, they were raised
above the head, and linked as if in a dance movement.
Then the left elbow was bent alongside the head, the
left hand resting on the left breast, and the right hand
on the right shoulder. As well as amputating the arms
in this version, Rodin severed the knees.

AUGUSTE RODIN
Large Head of Iris
1890-91, cast ?before 1913
Bronze
584 x 318 x 425
Lent by The Board of Trustees of the Victoria &
Albert Museum 1969
L00519

Large Head of Iris was first shown in Rome in March –
July 1913. In the catalogue to this exhibition it is
titled simply *Head*, but in Rodin's own list of the
works sent to Rome, he called it *Large Head of Demeter*. Demeter was the Greek Goddess of agriculture

and fertility.

This head exists in two smaller versions – one
bronze 10 cm high, and one terracotta 27 cm high,
both in the Musée Rodin. This last head is very similar to that of the *Crouching Woman* (opposite), which
was made as a study for the figure of *Iris, Messenger of
the Gods*, in the *Monument to Victor Hugo*.

Only one other bronze cast is known of the
enlargement: it is in the Musée Rodin. The cast
exhibited here was the one which went to Rome: it
has a label from the exhibition on the inside of the
neck.

AUGUSTE RODIN
Crouching Woman
1891
Bronze
540 x 940 x 440
Lent by The Board of Trustees of the Victoria &
Albert Museum 1993
L01698

This figure relates to Rodin's studies for the figure of Iris for a second, uncompleted version of his *Monument to Victor Hugo.* A photograph of the original plaster appears to show that the neck and back part of the head were made in a different plaster from the rest, and that the head may have been conceived separately from the torso and added later. *Crouching Woman* is an example of Rodin's practice of building a figure out of a collection of separate limbs, fused together rather than conceived as a whole. The right foot hangs in the air several inches higher than the rocky base of the sculpture, creating a dynamic disequilibrium in the figure. Rodin made an enlargement of the head, which is known as *Large Head of Iris* (opposite).

ARISTIDE MAILLOL
1861-1944

French sculptor, painter, lithographer, wood-engraver and tapestry designer, born at Banyuls in French Catalonia, near the Spanish border. Moved to Paris in 1881 to become a painter, and after four years was accepted at the Ecole des Beaux-Arts to study under Gérôme and Cabanel. Met Gauguin, whose belief in the importance of the decorative arts encouraged him to set up a tapestry studio at Banyuls. He began to make carved wooden sculpture in 1895, and took up sculpture full-time in 1900, when eye-strain forced him to stop making tapestry. He associated with the Nabis artists – Denis, Vuillard, Bonnard, Roussel and had his first one-man exhibition at the Galerie Vollard, Paris, 1902. In 1903 he started spending summers at his studio in Marly-le-Roi, near Paris, but went back to Banyuls every winter. He achieved recognition, and a reputation for classical and monumental sculptures of the female nude, when his first large statue, *The Mediterranean* was exhibited at the *Salon d'Automne* in 1905. He received many public commissions, including war memorials, and monuments to Cézanne and Debussy.

The Three Nymphs
1930-8, cast 1937-8
Lead
1575 x 1467 x 806
Presented by the National Art Collections Fund 1939
N05022

Maillol made the central figure of this group in 1930, modelled on Lucile Passavant, his pupil, who went on to become a distinguished sculptor and wood engraver. It was cast in plaster in February 1931, and reproduced in the magazine *Formes*, November 1931, as *Statue for a Group of the Three Graces*. While working on the group, however, the artist decided that they should be 'nymphs of the flowery meadows', rather than the Three Graces of classical mythology. 'They are too powerful to represent the Graces', he is reported to have said. At one stage in the making, the nymphs are said to have had their hands linked with a garland of flowers, and they are still crowned with daisies and buttercups.

Maillol's model, Lucile Passavant, recalled: 'Maillol wanted to sculpt the Three Graces and at his wish I went to Banyuls the following winter. He made there the central figure but his genius was monumental and although beautiful and radiant the clay despite everything resembled me. His Grace became a nymph, there ceased my collaboration as model. . . I believe he later completed the group with elements existing in his studio'.

The plaster version of the complete group was exhibited in June 1937 in the exhibition *The Masters of Independent Art 1895-1937* at the Petit Palais in Paris. It was still called *The Three Graces* then, and Maillol made further alterations to the figures over the next year, finishing the work in August 1938.

In May 1937, the National Art Collections Fund commissioned the central figure for presentation to the Tate, provided that a plaster cast was available for display at the opening of the new Duveen Sculpture Gallery on 20 June, 1937. The plaster was cast in lead in Paris in September and, at the request of the NACF, incorporated into the complete group of figures in December 1939.

Although two bronze casts exist, Maillol wanted the group to be cast in lead rather than bronze, as lead is lighter, and retains its original colour. Five lead casts are known, one of which originally stood in the sculptor's garden at Marly-le-Roi.

AUGUSTE RENOIR
1841-1919

French painter and sculptor, born in Limoges. Apprenticed to a painter of porcelain, and earned money to study art. Studied at the Ecole des Beaux-Arts in Paris under Charles Gleyre, and met Monet, Bazille, Sisley. He admired eighteenth-century painting, and his first works showed the influence of old master figure painting, as well as his interest in the non-academic methods of Delacroix and Courbet. Between 1869-74 he painted with Monet along the River Seine near Paris; they developed the style we know as Impressionism. Exhibited at Impressionist exhibitions 1874-82, and held his first one-man exhibition at *La Vie Moderne,* Paris, 1879. After visiting Italy in 1881, where he was impressed by Raphael and Pompeian frescoes, he turned away from Impressionism, developing a tighter, more precise drawing style influenced by Ingres, continuing to work primarily with the figure. He had always been interested in sculpture, but began to sculpt only very late in life, on the suggestion of his dealer, Ambroise Vollard, with the help of an assistant. Vollard introduced him to Guino, a young Catalan sculptor, who became his first assistant – by this time Renoir's hands were paralysed with arthritis. Guino had studied with Maillol, and was interested in making sculptures of classical female nudes.

After Renoir's death there were several important memorial exhibitions, and his late work also began to be appreciated.

Venus Victorious
1914, cast ?c1916
Bronze
1848 x 1118 x 775
Purchased 1950
N05934

Venus, the Goddess of love, holds an apple which in Greek mythology was given to her by Paris, the son of Priam, king of Troy. He was asked to judge who was the most beautiful of three Goddesses: Hera, wife of Zeus and queen of the heavens, Athene, Goddess of wisdom and war, and Venus.

Venus Victorious is the first large-scale sculpture Renoir made with his assistant, Guino, and he supervised every stage of the process. The figure was developed from a *Small Standing Venus* 60 cm high, modelled in 1913. The initial idea for these figures came from one of Renoir's earlier drawings. Renoir had classical figures of Venus in mind when he made the figure, and asked a friend to measure the proportions of a Greek female statue: 'Not the Venus de Milo, who is a big gendarme, but the Venus d'Arles or the Venus de Medici'. Renoir made sketches to change the expression of the head from the small statuette to the larger one; he also changed the drapery and used a different model, Maria, a young woman who often posed for him. Although he wanted the figure to be as alive and naturalistic as possible, he said he didn't want it to 'stink of the model'. They made a clay model, cast it in plaster, then worked further on the plaster outside in the garden, Renoir directing Guino's work with the aid of a pointing stick.

Renoir appears to have altered the work still further, after it had been cast in bronze, raising the breasts a little. The figure was first exhibited at *La Triennale* in Paris in March-April 1916, and was described as being the second cast of the first state. The cast exhibited, however, corresponds to one in the Petit Palais which is identified as being the final state.

Renoir intended to place the statue on a pedestal decorated with a relief depicting *The Judgement of Paris*, and Guino made such a relief based on Renoir's paintings of the same subject. Renoir quarrelled with Guino, however, and the relief was exhibited separately. Later, Renoir wanted the sculptor Marcel Gimond to make a 'Temple of Love' in his garden at Cagnes, in which to put his Venus, but this was never realised.

Guino and Claude Renoir, the artist's son, tried to make a copy in cement which Renoir wished to polychrome. However, each part was separately moulded and became out of shape, preventing them from piecing it together.

HENRI MATISSE
1869–1954

French painter, sculptor, lithographer, etcher and designer, born at Le Cateau Cambrésis. Studied law until taking up painting in 1890. Studied at the Ecole des Beaux-Arts in Paris under the Symbolist painter Gustave Moreau. He was influenced by Impressionism from around 1897. Under the influence of Signac, he began to use much brighter colours and was the leader of the group of painters known as the 'Fauves'. He started to make sculpture in 1901, and held his first one-man exhibition at the Galerie Vollard, Paris, 1904. Had his own art school in Paris 1908–11, but worked frequently in the South of France and visited Spain and Morocco. In late 1917 he moved to Nice. Designed sets and costumes for ballet, painted murals, and illustrated poetry in de luxe publications. In around 1948 he began to make work from cut, painted paper, and designed and decorated the chapel of the Rosary at Vence. Awarded the main painting prize at the 1950 Venice Biennale.

THE BACKS

The four *Backs* were made, at intervals, over a twenty-year period. They are the largest and most monumental sculptures of Matisse's career, and are one of the most important sculptural series in twentieth century art. Yet they were made, not as a commission, but for Matisse's own satisfaction. There is no indication that he intended them to be shown as a series: this was done for the first time in 1956, two years after his death, in the retrospective exhibition of Matisse's work at the Musée National d'art Moderne, Paris. That he kept returning to the series is an indication of the personal importance they had for him. All are on the same scale, slightly over life-size, and it is likely that Matisse used the plaster cast of each preceding version to make the next, simply adding clay to the plaster where he wanted to build it up.

There was one version, known as *Back 0*, which preceded all the others, made in 1909, and signed by Matisse, but never cast in bronze. It is known only from a photograph taken in 1909 before the clay was moved to the studio at Issy-les-Moulineaux. The modelling of the back and legs appears to have been

more flesh-like. *Back I* was probably made from this original clay.

They were cast in an edition of ten bronzes, plus one further cast for the artist's family.

The art critic Herbert Read suggested that: 'The series . . . summarises the complete evolution of Matisse's stylistic development in [sculpture]. The first *Back* is . . . naturalistic . . . the second is rather more summary or 'brutal', but there is no essential departure from the human model. But the third *Back*, which was apparently made immediately after the second, shows drastic simplifications of form. The limbs have become rigid trunks and a long 'tail' of hair descends from the head to balance the upward thrust of the legs. In the final version, which followed after an interval of fifteen years, the forms have become simplified to a degree rarely found in the paintings.'

Note on the purchase of *The Backs*

In March 1953 the Director of the Tate Gallery, John Rothenstein, wrote to Matisse to express interest in buying a bronze cast of a *Back* which had been on show in Battersea Park Exhibition in 1948, in plaster form.

Matisse replied, in June, that he would be happy to sell, but that there were three 'very different' versions, two of which were shown in Battersea, and asked which the Gallery was interested in. He added, however, that the bronze edition which he had (artist's proofs), had been bought by the Museum of Modern Art, New York, and he had none ready at that time. The Director replied later that month that they preferred the second version.

While negotiations were still in progress, in November 1954, Matisse died. By the end of the year his daughter, Marguerite Duthuit Matisse, had written to say that his family wished to carry out the artist's recent commitments.

Over the course of the next months, the Gallery began to consider buying not just the second stage, but what was then thought to be the complete set of three, and inquired in April 1955 if the family had copies of the other two, and what the cost would be.

Matisse's daughter repied that the family also considered the three bronzes to be a group, 'very indicative of the sculptural development of my father, although each one in itself represents the end of a particular stage. We would therefore be glad if in London as well as in New York, these three sculptures could be shown together'.

In June 1955 the Gallery informed the family of the Trustees' decision to buy all three works. When, however, the Director visited Paris later that month, he was shown *four* versions. The additional version (second in the series) had been discovered by the family in one of Matisse's old warehouse studios. The Gallery were offered all four at a reduced price of 11,000,000 francs (£11,000) to make possible the purchase of the complete series.

In August the Director made an appeal to the Treasury for additional funds to make the purchase. In October the request was refused. The Treasury suggested buying two only, with the option of buying the other two later, if funds permitted.

Having been informed of this disappointment, Matisse's daughter told the Gallery, in December, that she was happy to proceed on that basis, and that two were ready for collection from the Foundry. The Gallery decided to buy *Back I* and *Back IV* immediately, as these would stand alone from the set, better than *Back II* and *Back III*, should further funds not be forthcoming. The remaining two bronzes were lent until the Gallery eventually purchased the set, by launching a successful public appeal in 1956.

Back I
c 1909-10, cast 1955-6
Bronze
1899 x 1168 x 184
Purchased 1955
T00081

This, the first existing bronze *Back*, is closest to the model's pose: stood with her back to the artist, her left arm propped against the wall. The body has a loose, lumpy form; the muscles and sinews are pulled in different directions by the pose.

Matisse told the American curator Alfred H Barr Jr that this sculpture was made in Paris at the Boulevard des Invalides, where he had a studio and art school from the spring of 1908 until the summer of 1909. Madame Matisse believed, however, that it had been made in the studio at Issy-les-Moulineaux to which they had moved in the autumn of 1909.

The plaster for *Back I* was shown in Roger Fry's *Second Post-Impressionist Exhibition* at the Grafton Galleries, in London, in 1912, and then at the *Armory Show*, New York, in 1913.

Back II
c 1913-4, cast 1955-6
Bronze
1892 x 1206 x 190
Purchased with assistance from the Matisse Appeal Fund 1956
T00114

This relief was unknown until a few months after Matisse's death when it was found in a warehouse in Nice.

Back III
c 1916-7, cast 1955-6
Bronze
1880 x 1130 x 171
Purchased with assistance from the Matisse Appeal Fund 1957
T00160

This work, along with *Back IV* remained largely unknown until it was shown in Matisse's retrospective exhibitions in Lucerne and Paris in 1949 and 1950 (when it was identified as *Back II*). Matisse recalled that it was probably made before the 1914-8 war, but it has been dated on grounds of style to the period when he was working on the final state of *Bathers by a River,* in the Art Institute of Chicago. The left hand bather in the painting is close to this figure.

Back IV
1930, cast 1955-6
Bronze
1892 x 1130 x 159
Purchased with assistance from the Knapping Fund 1955
T00082

Matisse made this version shortly before his trip to Tahiti in the spring of 1930. Like *Back III* it was virtually unknown until the retrospective exhibitions of 1949 and 1950.

HENRI MATISSE
Back I
c 1909–10

28

HENRI MATISSE
Back II
c 1913–4

29

HENRI MATISSE
Back III
c 1916–7

HENRI MATISSE
Back IV
1930

31

HENRI MATISSE
Reclining Nude II
1927
Bronze
283 x 495 x 149
Purchased 1953
N04924

Matisse used this voluptuous pose in many of his paintings such as *The Joy of Life* 1905 and *The Blue Nude* 1907. He first used the pose for a sculpture in 1907 and took it up again twenty years later in this sculpture. Two years later he made a further version, *Reclining Nude III*.

Reclining Nude II was exhibited in Matisse's retrospective exhibition in Paris in 1950 alongside one of the other versions. It is closer in design to *Reclining Nude I* than to *Reclining Nude III*, and in this order the sculptures become progressively more abstract, as with the *Backs* series.

The sculptor William Tucker points to the usefulness of the pose: 'it was in the reclining figure that Matisse found the most satisfying solution: the reclining figure need not support itself by any but the most rudimentary anatomical structure; the problems of implied balance and muscular tension in the figure are avoided; the characteristic twist (Matisse's arabesque) can be the function of the structure as a whole, not of the pose (as with the standing figure)'.

The work was cast in bronze, in an edition of ten.

JACQUES LIPCHITZ
1891-1973

Sculptor, born in Lithuania, he moved to Paris in 1909, to study at the Ecole des Beaux-Arts, the Académie Julian and the Académie Colarossi. He collected 'primitive' and archaic art, was friendly with Picasso, and the Cubist artist Juan Gris, and the reliefs and sculptures he made from around 1914 are recognisably Cubist in style. His first one-man show was at the Galerie Léonce Rosenberg in Paris in 1920. In 1925-6 he developed his Cubist vocabulary of sculpted form to make open, transparent works, constructed from ribbons of metal. From around 1929 he began to sculpt allegorical, classical and biblical subjects, and he made a huge sculpture of *Prometheus* for the Paris International Exhibition in 1937. From 1941 he lived mainly in the United States, but spent his summers in Italy from 1963.

Reclining Woman with Guitar 1928, cast 1950s
Bronze
413 x 746 x 330
Purchased 1959
T00311

This sculpture was first made in black basalt, for the garden of the summer house at Le Pradet, designed by Le Corbusier for Mme de Mandrot. It was not large enough, so Lipchitz made it again in white stone.

The sculptor said that 'the curved shape of the right leg is also the shape of the guitar. This is again a total assimilation of the figure to the guitar-object; even the left arm reiterates the shape of the guitar. The work is massively conceived in curvilinear volumes, with a strong sense of frontality, but involving a movement in and out of depth'.

This is the third bronze cast, in an edition of seven. There was a study made in terracotta, and this has also been cast into bronze. The basalt version is now in the Museum of Modern Art, New York; the white stone version in the Kunsthaus, Zürich.

OSSIP ZADKINE
1890–1967

Sculptor, painter in watercolour and gouache, lithographer and tapestry designer, born in Smolensk, Russia. He went to Sunderland in 1905 to study English but studied art instead, moving to London in 1906 to study sculpture at Regent Street Polytechnic and the Central School, then briefly at the Ecole des Beaux-Arts in Paris. In 1911-2 he met Apollinaire, Brancusi, Archipenko, Lipchitz and Picasso, and made simplified figures, carved directly in wood and stone, influenced by Romanesque art and later by Cubism. Fought in the war, 1915-8. His first one-man exhibition was at the Galerie Le Centaure in Brussels, 1919. Around 1925 he began modelling sculpture to be cast in bronze. He spend the Second World War as a refugee in New York, and returned to Paris in 1945, where he taught and executed several public commissions, including a monumental figure to commemorate the bombing of Rotterdam, and a monument to Van Gogh at Auvers-sur-Oise. He was awarded the main sculpture prize at the 1950 Venice Biennale.

Venus
c 1922-4
Acacia wood
1918 x 533 x 464
Presented by F H Mayor as executor of the late
Richard Wyndham 1954
N06226

Zadkine described this figure as having been carved 'in an acacia tree', and the base takes the form of the tree-trunk from which the figure of Venus emerged. The sculptor identified this as one of the first works in which he reacted against Cubism.

The exact date of the sculpture is uncertain – Zadkine stated that the collector Richard Wyndham wanted to buy it when he first saw it in the sculptor's studio, but that he made him wait until he had seen it completed, in an exhibition. The figure was shown in Zadkine's first Paris exhibition, which was probably one at the Galerie Hodebert in 1925.

ALEXANDRE ARCHIPENKO
1887-1964

Russian-American sculptor, lithographer and teacher, born in Kiev, where he studied painting and sculpture. He moved to Paris in 1908, where he lasted only two weeks at the Ecole des Beaux-Arts. Instead he taught himself at the Louvre, looking particularly at Egyptian, Assyrian, archaic Greek and early Gothic work. He began to make very simplified, abstract sculptures, and then experimented with multi-media work, and complex constructions using found objects. Between 1912 and 1922 he made 'sculpto-paintings', a name he gave to reliefs made of plaster, carved and painted. He was associated with Cubism, and with the artists who exhibited together under the name 'Section d'Or': Picasso, Braque, Léger and Delaunay. His first one-man exhibition was at the Galerie Der Sturm, in Berlin in 1913, and in 1921 he moved to Berlin to teach. In 1923 he emigrated to New York, and set up his own art schools, where he taught. He wrote his *Polychrome Manifesto* in 1959.

Woman Combing her Hair
1915
Bronze
356 x 86 x 83
Purchased 1960
T00335

Archipenko called this work an example of the 'new concave', a sculpture in which negative, or concave volumes are combined with positive, convex elements, to create rhythmically complex work which he described as 'an entirely new and original type of sculpture with new aesthetic, optical and spiritual expressions'. Along with Brancusi, Archipenko developed a form of highly polished bronze sculpture, exemplified in this work.

This is the first version of this figure – Archipenko made a second version, 63.5cm high and a third, 180.5cm high. He also made a related sculpture, the same size as this one, called *Seated Woman Combing her Hair*, which shows a similar figure with both hands raised to her hair.

This cast appears to be dated 1914, but the other casts are either undated or dated 1915, and this is the date generally given to the work.

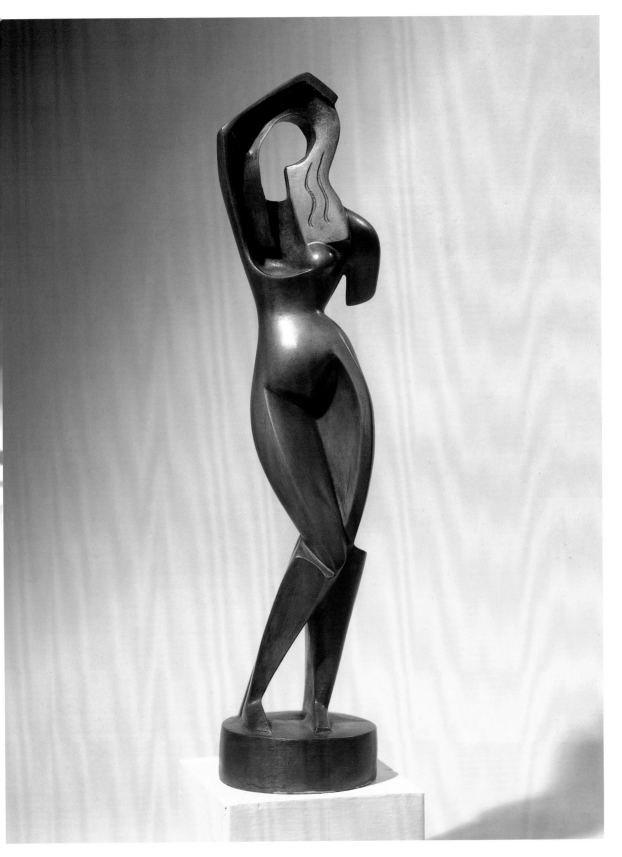

HENRI LAURENS
1885–1954

French sculptor and maker of *papiers collés* and prints, born in Paris. He learnt direct stone carving from an ornamental sculptor, and took evening classes from an academic sculptor known as 'Père Perin'. He met Braque in 1911, and knew Picasso and Gris. During the war he began to make *papiers collés* and still-life constructions in wood and iron, influenced by Cubism. In 1918 he started to make terracotta and later, bronze sculptures and reliefs, moving away from Cubist geometric form, towards a freer, more naturalistic style influenced by his friendship with Matisse and Maillol, and by the revival of classical styles after the war. In the 1930s his sculptures of women became extravagantly distorted and surreal in character, influenced perhaps by the work of Picasso in the late 1920s and early 1930s. Had a major retrospective exhibition at the Musée National d'art Moderne, Paris in 1951, and was awarded the *Grand Prix* at the 1953 São Paulo Bienal.

Autumn
1948, later cast
Bronze
762 x 1702 x 629
Purchased 1969
T01111

In the late 1930s and 1940s Laurens made several sculptures of nude female figures with titles such as *Morning, Night, Dawn* and *Summer. Autumn* is part of this group, and the title expresses the fullness and fruitfulness of the forms, with the suggestion that the figure is basking – ripening – in the sun. Claude Laurens, the son of the artist, remembers that the sculptures were only titled after they were finished, according to ideas suggested to the sculptor as he looked at them. Thus Laurens probably did not set out to make the hair look like leaves, but the resemblance may have prompted his choice of title.

The sculpture was developed from a smaller work, 50 cm long, which is very similar to the large figure, but is less finished.

BIBLIOGRAPHY

GENERAL READING

Breunig, Le Roy C, (ed), *Apollinaire on Art: Essays and Reviews 1902 - 1912*, New York, 1972

Clarke, Kenneth, *The Nude*, London, 1956, reprinted 1985

Elsen, Albert E, *Origins of Modern Sculpture: Pioneers and Premises*, New York, 1974

Elsen, Albert E, *Modern European Sculpture 1918 - 1945: Unknown Beings and Other Realities*, New York, 1979

Goldwater, Robert, *What is Modern Sculpture?*, New York, 1969

Nead, Lynda, *The Female Nude: Art, Obscenity and Sexuality*, London, 1992

Read, Herbert, *Modern Sculpture: A Concise History*, London, 1964, reprinted 1987

Rosenblum, Robert, *Cubism and Twentieth Century Art*, New York, 1959, reprinted 1976

Rubin, William, *'Primitivism' in Twentieth Century Art: Affinity of the Tribal and the Modern*, New York, 1989

Saunders, Gill, *The Nude: A New Perspective*, London, 1989

Tucker, William, *The Language of Sculpture*, London, 1977, reprinted 1988

Warner, Marina, *Monuments and Maidens: The Allegory of the Female Form*, London, 1987

BOOKS ON ARTISTS

Bork, Bert van, *Jacques Lipchitz: The Artist at Work*, New York, 1966

Busco, Marie, *Rodin and his Contemporaries*, London and New York, 1991

Butler, Ruth, *Rodin in Perspective*, New Jersey, 1980

Butler, Ruth, *Rodin, The Shape of Genius*, New Haven and London, 1993

Elsen, Albert E, *In Rodin's Studio: A Photographic Record of Sculpture in the Making*, London, 1980

Flanner, Janet, *Men and Monuments: Profiles of Picasso, Matisse, Braque and Malraux*, New York, 1990

Goldwater, Robert, *Lipchitz*, New York, 1959

Haesarets, Paul, *Renoir Sculptor*, New York, 1947

Hammacher, A A, *Jacques Lipchitz: his Sculpture*, New York, 1960

Hoffmann, Werner, *The Sculpture of Henri Laurens*, New York, 1992

Jianou, Ionel, *Zadkine*, Paris, 1964

Laurent, Monique, *Rodin*, London, 1990

Lipchitz, Jacques, and Arnason, H H, *My Life in Sculpture*, New York, 1972

Monneret, Sophie, *Renoir*, New Haven and London, 1993

Monod-Fontaine, Isabelle, *The Sculpture of Henri Matisse*, London, 1984

Stott, Deborah, *Jacques Lipchitz and Cubism*, New York, 1978

Vollard, Ambroise, *Renoir, an Intimate Record*, New York, 1990

Weldon, Huw (ed), *Monitor: an Anthology*, London, 1962 (includes interview with Zadkine)

EXHIBITION CATALOGUES

Rachael Adler Gallery, *Alexandre Archipenko: the creative process*, New York, 1993

Arts Council of Great Britain, *Rodin: Sculpture and Drawings*, London, 1987

Arts Council of Great Britain, *The Sculpture of Henri Matisse*, London, 1984

Smithsonian Institution, Washington, *Archipenko: International Visionary*, Washington, 1969

Museum of Modern Art, *Henri Matisse: A Retrospective*, New York, 1992

Tate Gallery, *The Lipchitz Gift: Models for Sculpture*, London, 1986